My Emotions
Mes émotions

CALM
LE CALME

A Crabtree Roots Book
Un livre de la collection Les racines de Crabtree

AMY CULLIFORD

Crabtree Publishing
crabtreebooks.com

School-to-Home Support for Caregivers and Teachers

This book helps children grow by letting them practice reading. Here are a few guiding questions to help the reader with building his or her comprehension skills. Possible answers appear here in red.

Before Reading:

- What do I think this book is about?
  - *This book is about feeling calm.*
  - *This book is about what feeling calm looks or feels like.*
- What do I want to learn about this topic?
  - *I want to learn what to do if I feel calm.*
  - *I want to learn what feeling calm looks like.*

During Reading:

- I wonder why...
  - *I wonder why we smile when we are calm.*
  - *I wonder why baths make people calm.*

What have I learned so far?
  - *I have learned that drawing can make you feel calm.*
  - *I have learned that people sit when they are calm.*

After Reading:

- What details did I learn about this topic?
  - *I have learned that there are many ways you can feel calm.*
  - *I have learned that you can think things through when you are calm.*
- Read the book again and look for the vocabulary words.
  - *I see the word **drawing** on page 4 and the word **music** on page 8. The other vocabulary words are found on page 14.*

Soutien de l'école à la maison pour les parents, les gardiens et les enseignants

Ce livre aide les enfants à se développer grâce à la pratique de la lecture. Voici quelques exemples de questions pour aider le lecteur ou la lectrice à développer ses capacités de compréhension. Les suggestions de réponses sont indiquées en rouge.

Avant la lecture

- De quoi ce livre parle-t-il?
  - *Ce livre parle du calme.*
  - *Ce livre explique à quoi ressemble le calme ou ce que l'on ressent.*
- Qu'est-ce que je veux apprendre sur ce sujet?
  - *Je veux apprendre ce qui rend les gens calmes.*
  - *Je veux apprendre à quoi ressemble le calme.*

Pendant la lecture

- Je me demande pourquoi...
  - *Je me demande pourquoi je souris quand je suis calme.*
  - *Je me demande pourquoi les bains calment les gens.*
- Qu'est-ce que j'ai appris jusqu'à présent?
  - *J'ai appris que dessiner peut me calmer.*
  - *J'ai appris que les gens s'assoient quand ils sont calmes.*

Après la lecture

- Nomme quelques détails que tu as retenus.
  - *J'ai appris qu'il existe plusieurs façons de se calmer.*
  - *J'ai appris que je peux réfléchir quand je suis calme.*
- Lis le livre à nouveau et cherche les mots de vocabulaire.
  - *Je vois le mot **dessiner** à la page 4 et le mot **musique** à la page 8. Les autres mots de vocabulaire se trouvent à la page 14.*

What makes you **calm**?

Qu’est-ce qui te **calme**?

Drawing makes me calm.

Dessiner me calme.

I sit when I am calm.

Je m’assois quand je suis calme.

Music makes me calm.

La **musique** me calme.

I can think when I am calm.

Je peux penser quand je suis calme.

A **bath** makes me calm.

Prendre un **bain** me calme.

I **smile** when I am calm.

Je **souris** quand je suis calme.

What makes you calm?

Qu'est-ce qui te calme?

Word List

Sight Words

a
am
can
I
makes
what
when
you

Liste de mots

Mots courants

je
peux
quand
qu’est-ce
suis
un

Words to Know
La boîte à mots

bath
bain

calm
calme

drawing
dessiner

music
musique

smile
souris

40 Words

What makes you **calm**?

Drawing makes me calm.

I sit when I am calm.

Music makes me calm.

I can think when I am calm.

A **bath** makes me calm.

I **smile** when I am calm.

What makes you calm?

39 mots

Qu'est-ce qui te **calme**?

Dessiner me calme.

Je m'assois quand je suis calme.

La **musique** me calme.

Je peux penser quand je suis calme.

Prendre un **bain** me calme.

Je **souris** quand je suis calme.

Qu'est-ce qui te calme?

My Emotions

CALM

Mes émotions

LE CALME

Written by/Autrice: Amy Culliford
Designed by/Conception: Rhea Wallace
Series Development/Développement des séries: James Earley
Proofreader/Relectrice: Ellen Rodger
Educational Consultant/Conseillère pédagogique: Marie Lemke M.Ed.

Photographs/Photographies:
Shutterstock: Juan Pablo Gonzaález: cover; ZouZou: p. 1; ESB Professional: p. 3, 14; LightField Studio: p. 5, 14; Africa Studio: p. 8, 14; Newman Studio: p. 9, 14; Chz_mhOng: p. 10, 14; narikan: p. 11, 14; Rusian Shugushev: p. 13

Crabtree Publishing

crabtreebooks.com 800-387-7650

 In Canada: We acknowledge the financial support of the Government of Canada through the Canada Book Fund for our publishing activities.

 Au Canada : Nous reconnaissons l'appui financier du gouvernement du Canada par l'entremise du Fonds du livre du Canada pour nos activités de publication.

Published in Canada
Publié au Canada
Crabtree Publishing
616 Welland Ave.
St. Catharines, Ontario
L2M 5V6

Published in the United States
Publié aux États-Unis
Crabtree Publishing
347 Fifth Avenue,
Suite 1402-145
New York, NY, 10016

Paperback 978-1-0398-5093-4
Ebook (pdf) 978-1-0398-5135-1
Epub 978-1-0398-5177-1

Printed in Canada/122023/CP20231116

Library and Archives Canada Cataloguing in Publication
Available at the Library and Archives Canada

Library of Congress Cataloging-in-Publication Data
Available at the Library of Congress